Marketing Strategies: Understanding Customer Relationship

OLAIDE EMMANUEL

Table of content

Chapter 1:**Generate leads**

A Beginner's Guide to Creating Business Leads the Inbound Way: Lead Generation
Discover how to start producing leads for your business in simple ways and how lead generation fits into your inbound marketing plan.

A lead is what?

Lead generation: What Is It?

Method for Generating Leads

A Lead's Qualification

Techniques for generating leads

A lead is what?
Every individual who expresses interest in a company's goods or services in any manner, shape, or form is considered a lead.

After initiating contact (by providing personal information for an offer, trial, or subscription), leads often hear from a company or organization. rather than receiving a random cold call from someone who bought their contact details.

Imagine you participate in an online survey to find out more about how to maintain your automobile. A few days later, the automaker that conducted the poll sends you an email with tips on how to take care of your vehicle. This procedure would be far less bothersome than if they had simply contacted you without any prior knowledge of your interest in auto repair, correct? This is what being a lead is like.

Moreover, from a business standpoint, the data the car firm gathers about you from your survey replies enables them to customise that initial conversation to meet your current issues — and not spend time phoning prospects who aren't at all interested in vehicle services.

Leads are a component of the larger lifecycle that customers go through when they go from being visitors to paying customers. Not every lead is created equally (nor are they qualified the same). Depending on how they are qualified and what stage of the lifecycle they are in, there are several sorts of leads.

Lead qualified for sales (SQL)
Contacts who have shown a clear interest in becoming paying clients are known as sales-qualified prospects. A contact who fills out a form to inquire about your product or service is an example of a SQL.

Product Qualified Lead (PQL) Contacts that have utilized your product and made actions that suggest interest in making a purchase are referred to as product qualified leads. PQLs are often used by businesses that provide free or restricted versions of their products with the opportunity to upgrade. Here is where your sales staff comes in.

A consumer who utilizes your free version yet interacts with or inquires about features that are only accessible via purchase is an example of a PQL.

Service Qualified Leads Contacts or clients who have communicated to your service staff their interest in becoming paying customers are known as service-qualified leads. A client who informs their customer service person that they would want to increase their product subscription is an example of a service-qualified lead; at this point, the customer service professional would up-level this client to the appropriate sales team or representative.

Lead generation: What is it?
The process of drawing potential customers to your company and piquing their interest via nurturing, with the ultimate objective of turning them into customers, is known as lead generation. Job applications, blog articles, discounts, live events, and online material are a few methods to create leads.

These lead generators are just a few examples of the lead generating techniques you may use to draw prospective clients and direct them toward your offerings. (We will discuss further tactics later.)

I can't just answer, "I develop content for lead generation," when someone from outside the marketing industry asks me what I do. They wouldn't get it at all, and I'd get some very bewildered stares.

Hence, I respond, "I try to come up with novel approaches to draw customers to my firm. I want to provide them just enough things to pique their interest in my business enough that they will ultimately want to hear from us."

Lead generation is a method of introducing prospective clients to your brand and setting them on the route to ultimately completing a purchase, and that is often what resonates best.

Why is lead generation necessary?

The change from a stranger to a consumer is far more natural when a stranger approaches you by expressing a genuine interest in your company.

The second step of the inbound marketing process is called lead generation. When you've garnered a following and are prepared to turn those viewers into leads for your sales team, it happens (namely sales-qualified leads).

As seen in the picture below, generating leads is an important step on the road to becoming a satisfied client.

The three Cs of lead generation: Cease, Conceal, and Delight

Method for Generating Leads

Let's go through the lead generation process' phases now that we are aware of how lead generation fits into the inbound marketing technique.

A visitor first learns about your company via one of your marketing platforms, including your website, blog, or social media profile.

A call-to-action (CTA) is a picture, button, or message that prompts website visitors to take some form of action. This visitor then clicks on your CTA.

Its CTA directs the user to a landing page, a web page created with the purpose of collecting lead information in return for an offer. A landing page's "offer" is the content or valuable item that is being made available. This may be a template, an ebook, or a course.

Your visitor submits a form on the landing page in return for the offer.

See how it all works together?

Marketing for lead generation
After you've assembled all of these components, you can start producing leads by using your different advertising channels to direct people to your landing page.

But which platforms need to you use to advertise your landing page? Let's discuss lead generation marketing, which is the first stage of lead generating.

This flow chart demonstrates how promotional marketing channels lead to produced leads if you learn best visually.

ways for generating leads, This flow diagram illustrates how a lead is created via promotional marketing outlets.

Many more avenues exist for converting site users into leads. Let's discuss a few more and go into further detail about them.

The best technique to direct readers to a landing page is via content. Usually, the purpose of content creation is to provide free, helpful information to readers. CTAs may be placed wherever in your content, including inline, at the bottom of the article, in the hero, and even on the side panel.

A visitor is more likely to click your call-to-action and go to your landing page if they are more pleased with your content.

Email Email is a terrific way to connect with customers who are already familiar with your company, brand, and offerings. Because they have already joined your mailing list, asking them to do anything is considerably simpler.

Since emails are often crowded, utilize CTAs with attention-grabbing designs and intriguing language to draw subscribers in.

The Simple Way to Retargeting and Email Marketing
An advertisement's only goal is to persuade viewers to act. Why spend the money if not?

Make sure your landing page and offer perfectly match what is promised in the advertisement and that the action you want consumers to take is obvious if you want them to convert.

Blog

It's a nice thing that you may customize the whole article to the final objective when utilizing your blog posts to advertise an offer.

You may create a blog article on how to choose your marketing metrics if your offer is a video tutorial on how to set up Google Search Console. It would make your CTA really clickable and relevant.

Trials of Products

By allowing people to try out your product or service before buying it, you may remove several obstacles to a transaction. After a potential customer has started using your product, you may lure them with further offers or helpful information to persuade them to purchase.

Including your logo in your free versions as another excellent practice to attract more prospective consumers.

Affiliate Marketing

In a different approach, word-of-mouth marketing and referrals are helpful for lead generation. That is, it raises the likelihood that you will get more leads by getting your brand in front of more people.

Regardless of the lead generation method you use, you should direct consumers to your landing page. Everything else will fall into place as long as you've created a landing page that converts.

Content, emails, adverts, blogs, social media, product trials, and referral marketing are all examples of lead generating marketing.

Why not just purchase leads?

Both marketers and salespeople want to swiftly load their sales funnels with prospects. Enter the lure of lead purchases.

First and foremost, none of the leads you've bought have ever met you. They usually "opted in" while signing up for anything at another website, but they didn't really want to hear from your business.

Your communications with them are consequently unwelcome, and sending such communications is invasive. (Recall that annoying remember I received when I was attempting to eat my spaghetti? People experience this when they get emails and other communications from someone they didn't invite to contact them.)

If a potential customer has never visited your website and has shown interest in your goods or services, you are just interrupting them.

There's a good risk they could mark your communications as spam if they never agreed to receive messages from you explicitly.

You are added to a "blacklist," which is then shared with other email providers after enough people report your communications as spam. It's quite difficult to come off the blacklist after you've been put on it. Also, your IP reputation and email deliverability may probably suffer.

Always, always, always choose organic lead generation over buying leads. Instead of purchasing an email list, read this blog article to discover how to build one.

A Lead's Qualification

A lead is a person who has shown interest in the goods or services offered by your business, as was discussed in the first section. Let's now discuss how someone may truly demonstrate their interest.

Information gathering is what creates a sales lead. Many methods might be used to gather the information.

Maybe a candidate for a job expresses interest in the position by applying. Maybe a customer exchanges contact details for a voucher. Maybe someone fills out a form to download some instructional material.

Detecting the Degree of Interest in a Lead
These are just a handful of the many methods you may use to qualify a lead. Each of these instances demonstrates how a lead's degree of interest and the quantity of information gathered to qualify them might differ.

Let's evaluate each situation:

Job Application: To be considered for a post, a person must be ready to provide a great deal of personal data on an application form. Filling out the application demonstrates their genuine interest in the position, which qualifies them as a lead for the hiring staff at the organization rather than the marketing or sales teams.

Coupon: Unlike a job application, likely, you don't know much about someone who finds one of your internet coupons. Yet, if they think the offer is worthwhile enough, they may be prepared to swap their name and email address for it. Even if there isn't much information, it's plenty for a firm to understand that there is interest in their brand.

Content: Unlike coupons, which demonstrate a person's direct interest in your goods or service, content (such as an informative ebook or webinar) does not. As a result, you'll probably need to gather additional information to fully grasp the nature of the person's interest in your company before you can decide if they're a good match and whether they're interested in your product or service.

These three instances illustrate how lead generation varies from business to business and from individual to individual.

The amount of data that you need to gather will depend on the nature of your company to determine if someone has a genuine interest in your product or service.

One example of a question to include in a lead generation form is this:

Full Name: The most basic piece of information required to tailor your correspondence with each lead.

Email: You will contact your lead using this as a unique identifier.

Firm and website: This will enable you to investigate the industry and business of your lead and determine whether or not they might benefit from your offering (mainly for B2B).

Business Size: The more information you can get in-depth while maintaining conversion rates, the better. Your leads might be further qualified if you are aware of their employment count.

See our article on information collecting and what to ask for on lead generation forms if you're interested in further intermediate-level advice.

scoring first

Lead scoring is a method of quantitatively qualifying leads. With this approach, leads are given a numerical value (or score) to assess where they lie on the spectrum from "interested" to "ready for a sale".

You are entirely free to set the standards for these acts, but they must be the same in both your marketing and sales divisions so that everyone is operating on the same scale.

The parameters used by your sales team to generate a lead's score may include the activities they have performed, the information they have supplied, how engaged they are with your brand, or other factors. For instance, you may give someone a better rating if they interact with you often on social media or if their demographics fit your target market.

Using the examples from the above, you could give a lead a better score if they used one of your coupons since doing so would indicate that they are enthusiastic about your offerings.

The closer a leader is to a sales-qualified lead (SQL), which is only one step away from becoming a customer, the better their lead score. You should experiment with the scoring criteria until you discover the right combination. After you do, your lead generation will change into customer generation.

Techniques for generating leads
Depending on the platform you choose to use to gather leads, there are a variety of approaches, campaigns, and strategies that go under the umbrella of online lead generation. We discussed the best ways to collect leads after a site visitor has arrived. but, how do you first get them there?

Let's explore lead-generation tactics for a few well-known platforms.

Instagram Lead Generation
From its conception, Facebook has been used to generate leads.

Initially, businesses could leverage information from their biographies and outbound links in their articles to attract new visitors to their websites. Nevertheless, there was a significant change in how companies utilized the network to get leads once Facebook Advertising was introduced in 2007 and its algorithm started to favor accounts that employed sponsored advertising.

For this reason, Facebook developed Lead Advertising. Moreover, Facebook has a tool that enables you to add a straightforward call-to-action button at the top of your Facebook Page, which may be used to link Facebook users to your website.

Obtain some Facebook lead-generating advice.

Twitter Lead Generation 50 Facebook Ad Examples That We Clicked
With Twitter Lead Gen Cards, you can create leads inside a tweet without ever leaving the platform. Users just need to click "Submit" to enter their lead information, which includes their name, email address, and Twitter username.
How to Utilize Twitter for Business and a Template for Follower Tracking
generating leads on LinkedIn

From its inception, LinkedIn has grown its involvement in the advertising sector. In terms of lead generation, LinkedIn developed Lead Gen Forms that, when a user clicks a CTA, automatically fill up information from their profile.

Learn from our LinkedIn advertising expertise.

Lead generation using PPC
Pay-per-click (PPC) advertisements are those that appear on search engine result pages (SERPs). With 3.5 billion searches every day, Google is an excellent location for any advertising campaign, particularly lead generation.

The success of your PPC campaign primarily depends on your budget, your target keywords, and a few other elements in addition to a smooth user flow.

Read more about setting up effective PPC advertising.

Creating B2B Leads

A unique strategy to lead generation is necessary for the B2B business model. Referrals are the best option for obtaining company leads, according to SmartInsights. In addition, efficacy varies depending on the channel.

Discover how to generate B2B leads with each channel.

Recommendations for Lead Generation Campaigns

There might be a lot of moving pieces in a lead generation effort at any given time. It might be challenging to determine which elements of your campaign are effective and which need some adjustments.

What precisely goes into the finest lead-generating engine in its class? Here are some pointers for creating lead-generation campaigns.

Observe your data.

Start with the wealth of data you currently have at your disposal if you're trying to develop a lead-generating engine. Start by saving the articles that often score well, drive traffic, and relate to your product.

You can decide where to put CTAs after you understand what works successfully.

AJ Beltis, a senior marketing manager at HubSpot who focuses on media conversion, advises, "With these posts, ask yourself what the missing middle element is between what someone is reading about and what you can provide them. If the material is aimed at those farther along in the purchase cycle, it may be a demo, an in-depth explanation, or even an actionable template.

Keep in mind that your CTA shouldn't deviate too much from the post's subject.

Make it simple and logical, advises Beltis, and the leads will pour in.

Use the appropriate lead-generating tools.
The most effective marketing teams employ a formal method to arrange and keep their leads, as you can see from our statistics. Lead-generating software and solutions are useful in this situation.

How much information do you have on the users of your website? Do you have their email addresses or names? What about the sites they browsed, their navigational patterns, and their actions both before and after submitting a lead conversion form?

You're likely having trouble connecting with site visitors if you don't know the answers to these questions. You should be able to respond to these queries, and you may do so by using the appropriate lead-generation tools.

You may generate several lead generation assets to utilize on your website using a variety of tools and templates:

CTA Templates: Create clickable call-to-action (CTA) buttons for your blog, landing pages, and other areas of your website with these 50+ free, editable PowerPoint templates.

Tools for Lead Generation: This HubSpot free tool has lead capture and contact insights tools that can scrape any pre-existing forms on your website and add the contacts to your current contact database. Moreover, it enables you to construct "lead flows," which are pop-ups, hello bars, or slide-ins that help you convert website visitors into leads right away.

A slide-in lead flow example.

Tracing visitors to an image source: A heatmap tool from Hotjar generates a colored illustration of how a person moves across your website. You may better understand user behavior on your site with this information.

Form-Scraping Tool: A form-scraping tool allows you automatically compile all of your leads into your contact database by gathering submissions on the current forms on your website. Customers of HubSpot may design and integrate forms that your CRM will then automatically fill out. To automatically add submissions to a contact database, non-HubSpot clients may create forms using a platform like Contact Form 7 or Google Forms and then utilize HubSpot's free collected forms service.

Make incredible offers for all phases of the purchasing cycle.

Not every visitor to your website is prepared to speak with your sales staff.

A customer who is in the early stages of the buying process could be interested in an educational resource like an ebook or a guide, while a buyer who is closer to the end of the process and is already acquainted with your business would be more interested in a free trial or demo.

Make sure you develop offers for every stage and provide CTAs for these offers all around your website.

True, it takes time to develop educational material that nurtures leads through the sales funnel, but if you don't provide anything for website visitors who aren't ready to make a purchase, they may never return. Here are 23 suggestions for lead-generation material to get you started, ranging from checklists and templates to free tools.

Try employing clever CTAs if you want to go beyond customization and increase your conversion rate. Whether a person is a new visitor, a lead, or a customer, smart CTAs can determine where they are in the buyer's journey and show CTAs appropriately.

Maintain consistency in your message and fulfill your commitment.
Lead-generation programs that deliver on their promises have the best conversion rates.

Provide value to everyone who interacts with your lead acquisition process and make sure your messaging is consistent throughout.

The elements of your campaign have to be the same as everything else on your website, blog, and final product that you'll attempt to sell. If not, moving your lead to the next lifecycle stage will be challenging.

You should have more goals for your campaign than merely collecting email addresses. You should work to get new clients.

Your CTA should go to a specific landing page. You would think this is simple, but you'd be astonished at how few marketers make specific landing pages for their offers. The purpose of CTAs is to direct users to a landing page where they may access a particular offer.

Don't, for instance, utilize CTAs to direct visitors to your homepage. You should still direct them to a landing page that is relevant to their search even if your CTA is about your brand or product (and maybe not an offer like a download).

Send them to a page that will turn them into a lead if you have the chance to employ a CTA.

Download our booklet on optimizing landing pages for conversions to discover more about how to create and market high-converting landing pages.

Participate with your sales team.
Remember how we discussed lead scoring? However, without the assistance of your sales staff, it cannot be done.

The definitions and steps involved in converting a lead from MQL to SQL to opportunity must be agreed upon by both your marketing and sales departments.

Be willing to change how you interact with sales and how you move prospects through your funnel. You'll probably need to hone your definitions over time. Just be sure to keep all parties informed.

Make smart use of social media.
As mentioned in the lead gen tactics above, social media may still be a valuable and affordable source for lead generation, although marketers often see it as ideal for top-of-the-funnel marketing.

Start by including links in your Facebook, Twitter, LinkedIn, and other social media postings that go straight to the landing pages of effective offers.

Inform site visitors that they are being sent to a landing page. You're creating expectations in this manner. Here's an example from one of our tweets:

a HubSpot tweet regarding certification in digital marketing

Picture Source

You should make it a point to consistently connect social media postings to your most successful blog entries after doing a lead generation audit of your site to see which ones produce the most leads.

Running a contest is another technique to get leads from social media. Contests may educate you a lot about your audience while also being entertaining and engaging for your followers. Win-win situation.

Make use of your collaborations.
Co-marketing may be effective for generating leads. If your team collaborates with other businesses, pool your resources to develop some offerings that will benefit both parties.

According to Jasmine Fleming, marketing manager at HubSpot, "in the Content Offers team, we conduct campaigns with partner organizations that have a similar target demographic and brand values to generate and promote gated material like ebooks, reports, and templates.

According to Fleming, the offer generates leads for both HubSpot and our partners. We may trade leads among us, she suggests. Co-marketing offerings can provide a lot more leads than a piece of content produced by one firm alone.

Keep an open mind and iterate often.
Your lead generation approach must be as flexible as the audience you are trying to reach. Trends, practices, and attitudes all change throughout time. Furthermore, your lead generation marketing should.

To find out which landing pages convert better, which CTAs work better, and which text best engages your target audience, use A/B split testing.

To identify what works, try out different layout modifications, design, UX, content, and advertising channels.

Benchmarks & Trends in Lead Generation
Hence, you're generating leads and website visitors. So how do you do in comparison to other businesses in your sector?

Continue reading to see how other marketers are using lead generation in 2023, along with significant statistics to take into account.

The main focus of marketing is lead generation. According to the HubSpot State of Marketing Report 2021, creating more leads is marketers' #1 marketing concern. According to SmartInsights, converting these leads into clients is another top goal.

Referrals are the main source of B2B leads. According to B2B marketers, 38% of their leads originate from emails, 65% from referrals, and 33% from SEO (SEO).

If you want to capitalize on this trend, you need to rethink your referral approach and encourage current clients to recommend you to others.

Using content marketing to generate leads.
Marketers claim that during the previous 12 months, content marketing has effectively assisted them in generating demand and leads. Read this useful blog article on developing content for various phases of the buyer's journey to capitalize on this trend.

Gain Strength Through Lead Generation
There you go, people. We advise you to test HubSpot's free lead-generating tool now that you are more knowledgeable about how to produce leads for your company. Use it to add simple conversion assets to your website (or scrape the data from your current forms) so you can learn more about your site visitors and the kind of content that encourage conversions.

The fundamentals that we covered in this blog article are only the start. Continue to develop excellent offers, CTAs, landing pages, and forms, and market them in multi-channel settings. Be in continuous contact with your sales staff to ensure that you are consistently transferring high-quality leads.

Also, never stop testing. You can enhance lead quality and boost revenue by adjusting and testing each stage of your inbound lead creation process.

Chapter 2:**Choose your target**

Why is it crucial to know who your target market is?

You'll obtain better results from your marketing efforts after you've identified your target market. To understand why it is necessary to define "target audience."

Regardless of whether you call them your target audience, target market, or intended audience, this group of people is the audience most likely to like your product or service. You can reach these two goals by performing your research and identifying your target market:

You'll stop assuming what your target market is going to be. It's easy to assume that people who are interested in your product are similar to you, but audience numbers are the only way to be certain. The audience definition research will identify the real traits and passions of your target group.

You will be aware of the marketing materials to develop for your customers. You may produce content and other marketing materials that are relevant to your audience by understanding their preferences and problems.

These benefits will increase the possibility that you will earn more money by making it easier to conduct marketing that resonates with your target audience. After all, viewing your advertisement is one thing, but benefiting from it is a very other stories.

What Are Good Questions to Ask About Your Target Audience?

While choosing your target market, keep the following questions at the forefront of your mind:
They — who? You must comprehend the traits of your target audience to create marketing that will appeal to them.

What are the most urgent problems that your organization can resolve there? Knowing your audience's problems can help you pitch your product as the solution to their problems.

What kind of things do they like? Consider the kind of content your target audiences like so you can advertise utilizing related themes and subjects.

Where do they go to pass the time, both online and offline? You may place your marketing materials for maximum exposure by understanding where your target population consumes marketing.

Who are you marketing to?

If you are unable to do so right away, you must first decide who your target market is. Marketing that works targets, specific customers. By being aware of these individuals, you may carry out marketing to the fullest extent possible.

You'll obtain better results from your marketing efforts after you've identified your target market. To understand why it is necessary to define "target audience."

Regardless of whether you call them your target audience, target market, or intended audience, this group of people is the audience most likely to like your product or service. You can reach these two goals by performing your research and identifying your target market:

You'll stop assuming what your target market is going to be. It's easy to assume that people who are interested in your product are similar to you, but audience numbers are the only way to be certain. The audience definition research will identify the real traits and passions of your target group.

You will be aware of the marketing materials to develop for your customers. You may produce content and other marketing materials that are relevant to your audience by understanding their preferences and problems.

These benefits will increase the possibility that you will earn more money by making it easier to conduct marketing that resonates with your target audience. After all, viewing your advertisement is one thing, but benefiting from it is a very another story.

What Sorts of Target Markets Are There?

Using characteristics from their life experiences, tastes, and purchasing habits, you may determine your target audience. Segmentation is a technique used by certain marketers that are adept at understanding their audience to separate them into groups depending on these characteristics. Just keep in mind that at this stage of the process, you may assess your audience using groups like these target market demographic examples:

Age\sGender\sCareer\sLocation

Subculture

Opinions and attitudes

Buying Intention (likelihood to buy your product)

Interests and passions
Lifestyle

How Do You Do Audience Research?

Even while it may seem overwhelming to get to know a huge number of individuals, there are several straightforward approaches you may use. Most crucially for small enterprises, the majority of these techniques are free or inexpensive.
Take a Customer and Content Reader Survey

Are you curious about your audience? Query them directly. Use the audience survey template you obtained at the beginning of this article and proceed as follows:
Create survey objectives. List the top five things you want to discover from your survey about your audience.
Choose a survey platform. Some well-liked free and inexpensive choices are SurveyMonkey, Google Forms, and Crowdsignal.
Make up the survey questions. Attempt to maintain a connection between them and the list

you made in the first stage. Asking your audience about their demographics, internet habits, and brand experiences could be a good idea.

Choose a due date for your survey. We recommend allowing two weeks to a month to allow for those who are unable to answer straight away.

Use your most popular outlets to promote your survey. Try promoting it on your website, posting it on social media, or emailing it to your list.

If you have the ability, provide incentives to those who complete your survey. You may provide a manual or resource, branded merchandise, a coupon code, or a chance to enter a drawing.

Interview Your Existing Clients

One-on-one interviews provide greater data about specific customers' experiences compared to customer surveys, which just provide general information about the individuals who appreciate your product. These chats will provide you with rich emotional information that will help you understand why your clients interact with your brand.

When you prepare for and conduct your customer interviews, keep the following advice in mind:

Establish a specific objective for your interview: Have a goal for your interview that your questions will relate to, just as you did with your customer survey.

Utilize open-ended inquiries: Using open-ended questions rather than closed-ended ones yields better results, as we discussed in our guide to interviewing subject matter experts. For instance, asking a consumer, "Tell me how you prefer to use our product," can elicit more information from them than asking, "Do you find our product useful?"

Be receptive: In their guide to customer interviews, HubSpot notes that it's OK for a customer to sometimes criticize your product. These responses will assist you in discovering what your audience dislikes and how to enhance their overall experience.

Finish with a tried-and-true journalistic tip: Since you and your client are both people with unique views on life, your inquiries will fall short of covering all your consumer wants to say. Because of this, a lot of journalists would ask, "Would you want to add anything that I haven't inquired about in this interview?" This question often yields some of the most perceptive responses for journalists who utilize it.

Before conducting your interview, jot down your questions using the form you obtained from our target audience package. For additional insights on interviewing customers, download our entire guide to customer interview best practices.

Verify Your Google Analytics Population Statistics

Google Analytics keeps track of demographic information on the location, interests, gender, and age of visitors to your website. Go to Demographics overview or Demographic information under User by selecting the Reports option from the left-hand menu.

a sample of the Google Analytics demographics overview page

To access information on your demographics' engagement and conversion rates, go to the Demographics details tab or click the link in the bottom right corner of each box on the Demographics overview page. Even if a large number of individuals may visit your website at once, they may not be the most interested visitors. Verify which audience groups are reading and responding to the information on your website.

Turn on Google signals in your data settings if you don't see demographic information on your Analytics dashboard.

Get Audience and Demographic Information from Social Media

The majority of the main social networking sites keep track of your followers' basic demographic information. Discover where to look for that information on each site:

Navigate to Facebook Business Suite, choose Insights from the left-hand menu, then select the Audience tab to access Facebook/Instagram.

Employ a third-party application; Twitter no longer offers a built-in dashboard for audience statistics.

Visit Followers in the Analytics section of LinkedIn Pages.

In the Analytics menu, choose Audience Insights on Pinterest.

These social media demographics include information on the audience's age, gender, and even level of experience.

Use Market Research Companies for Data

Market research business reports will provide you with a general overview of the populations that utilize your goods. Although hiring a market research company to examine your particular target may be out of your small business price range, these companies often sell or share research results.

These are two instances of public audience insights from well-known brands. This free research from Nielsen examines Black Americans' perceptions of marketing representation. To assist you to understand what marketing trends consumers react to, Gartner offers annual marketing forecasts.

Are you unsure of where to locate market research firms that are relevant to your audience and sector? An overview of the market research sector and some of its most well-known players can be found on Software Testing Help.
Assess the Data from Your Existing Customers

You probably already have consumer information that can help your audience research efforts. What of these sources of client data do you have access to?

a client database using customer relationship management (CRM) software or a comparable system
history of consumer purchases
Details about email list subscribers
Review of businesses and products

Even something as basic as an invoice may provide you with information about how your present clients engage with your company.
Implement social listening

Searching for keyword mentions on websites or in social media is known as social listening. These terms, including your brand name, often have something to do with your company or sector. You may do specific keyword searches on each site you watch or utilize specialized social listening software.

Watch out for terms like Your brand name.
the brands of your rivals
titles of your original goods or services
your company's name

Keep an eye out for the themes and problems that individuals bring up as you listen to how they discuss these issues. Are your target audience members looking for anything fresh in your industry? What do they laud or criticize?

See Your Most Popular (and Least Popular) Content

Analyze the metrics for your blog entries to see which subjects and strategies are most effective with your readers. Page views and bounce rates provide some useful information, but content analytics provide much more useful data. Consider measurements such as:

Rate of clicks through Readership response to your blog post's call to action

Average page view time: The typical amount of time people spend on a blog post's page

Conversion rate: The proportion of readers who take your call to action to those who visit your blog content.

You may use your favorite analytics software to look at these figures or do a thorough content audit, depending on how much time you have.

Identify More Material That Your Audience Reads

Your brand is merely one of the content sources available to your audience. On what additional businesses and publications may they rely? What subjects interest and inform them?

Examine the following to see what other writings your audience reads:
material of your rivals
material that is popular in your sector
content that is well-liked by the people in your social network circles
Trending industry content on BuzzSumo

How Do You Know Who Your Target Audience Is?

You'll have a significant quantity of audience information to utilize after performing the actions we just discussed. How can you determine what this data indicates about your audience, then? An examination of your target audience may be done as follows.

Analyze Your Data for Recurring Themes

Look closely at your data for trends in the target audience categories we discussed at the start of this piece, such as:

Interests

gender and age

Career\sIncome

Problems and obstacles that your product may help with

Liveliness and interests

preferred content

Internet use patterns

Purchasing customs

While you search for commonalities with your audience, have an open mind. Even the smallest details, like a preferred website or language choice, may provide you insight into your client's marketing preferences.

Create customer personas from your data

Use the insights you gained from your data to develop marketing personas, which are fictitious representations of your average consumer. When attempting to match your marketing to your audience, these tools provide a fantastic target audience example.

A marketing persona contains information such as A picture or illustration of the hypothetical consumer
Name and title Information on demographics, such as age, gender, income level, and education
Interests and passions
product-related objectives and problems
Values and concerns about your product
preferred content providers

All of this information can be found in the marketing persona template that you downloaded at the start of this blog article.
How Can You Utilize Audience Information in a Marketing Plan?

It's time to use the information you now have about your target audience.

Make marketing materials that are aimed toward your target market's personas.

From this point on, your marketing should be guided by your target audience information and client profiles. Several elements of your marketing materials should be influenced by the information you have about your audience:

Copy: While writing, use language that seems natural to the readers. For instance, if you're selling an executive-targeted business-to-business product, you should use more professional, sales-oriented language than your normal business-to-customer audience would like. When in doubt, speak in the manner of your audience.

Topics: Include subjects in your content that relate to the junction between your audience's interests and your product.

Design: Employ visual components that reflect the tastes and experiences of your target audience. A lot of primary colors could be used, for instance, if you sell to children and their parents.

Provide Solutions to the Issues Your Audience Has

You discovered the issues your clients have and the issues your product can address when you conducted audience research and created marketing personas. Consider your product's solutions while you write your marketing text and content. Use the following techniques to create marketing text that is solution-focused:

Identify the issue your client is having and connect with them.

Point out how your product's main advantage relates to your client's most pressing issue.

Provide a specific illustration of how your product may benefit a consumer.

Show off your differentiator - the one method you can address the issue for your consumer that your rivals cannot.

Wherever Your Audience Travels, Repurpose Your Content

After you've produced content that resonates with your target market, repurpose it for use across many platforms to get the most out of it. To put it another way, arrange your content for another marketing channel (such as social media, email, etc.) before sharing it there.

You might, for instance, transform a blog article into:
A podcast conversation
a video explanation
An email bulletin
a thread on Twitter
a graphic info

As part of your social media content strategy, don't forget to often share your material.
Make Marketing Efforts That Draw in Your Audience

You may safely proceed to produce particularly customized marketing for your audience after you have the facts about your target audience in hand. To maintain your marketing focus, don't forget to include a review of your target audience in processes like your content development process.

Chapter 3:**Find you clients**

Beyond creating a product, the first step in starting any firm is locating the first client. And doing that is far simpler stated than done.

Many firms fail right away because the drive to start making money takes priority over all of the planning and product development. It seems harder than you anticipated to convince that first customer to part with their money, and you start to question what you're doing incorrectly.

1. Inform yourself

The first step in attracting customers is to understand your market. Do the essential inquiries to fully comprehend your sector and the items or services that prospective customers are seeking. No matter how skilled a salesman you are, it won't matter if you aren't providing the correct goods.

Determine what you can provide that would fill a niche and outperform your rivals by doing a comprehensive analysis of the competition. Be willing to accept the possibility that your first creation needs refinement. Continue to study and concentrate on meeting the demands of your clientele.

2. Establish a presence online

Nowadays, acquiring your first customer is almost difficult without a significant web presence. You need to engage with prospective customers on social media and have a website that looks professional. Customers need a method to learn more about you on their own and a way to get in touch with you.

Platforms for simple yet expert website design, such as Wix and Squarespace, may assist you in quickly launching a quality website.

Use social media.

Social media is one of the most significant marketing mediums nowadays.

You are passing up a lot of chances to build your brand, engage with new clients, and generate leads if you aren't utilizing Facebook, Twitter, LinkedIn, or Instagram.

Create or join a social media group that is focused on a topic related to your company, and utilize this to engage and gain the confidence of potential customers.

Put engagement first. For instance, if you offer hair care products, ask other members of the Facebook group for their top hair care advice and add your own.

4. Internet

Nothing beats networking when it comes to acquiring new customers. And doing so entails moving beyond social media. Attend industry-related events like seminars and conferences and make as many new contacts as you can. Too many individuals just depend on the internet world when deciding where to obtain customers.

Be brazen in your self-promotion; in fact, be shameless. Discover a means to have real, face-to-face encounters, even if doing so may be challenging in a post-pandemic environment.

Never wait too long to follow up after networking with someone. If you wait a few months before contacting them once again, they may have forgotten who you are and you will have lost your opportunity.

5. Employ inbound advertising
Employ pull marketing or inbound marketing to attract customers to your website and raise your brand's exposure. You may do this by creating keyword-rich content in your area of expertise using best practices for search engine optimization (SEO), or you can cross-promote with a similar website.

Blog postings or YouTube videos that educate prospective clients are some types of material you may utilize for this campaign. You may produce a series of movies demonstrating hair care advice, for instance, if you offer hair care products. Personal pet

Managing relationships and developing a personal connection with individuals are the keys to finding customers. If you have identified someone who has shown interest in your company, get to know them and learn about their requirements.

Invest yourself wholeheartedly in finding a solution. Determine any areas of weakness you can strengthen, show your knowledge of the issue, and be affable and supportive.

This raises the likelihood that your first customer will purchase from you by fostering demand for the goods and confidence in you.

To be ready for future meetings, make notes on the requirements of certain prospects and other relevant information. They'll be awed by your memory and more inclined to believe in you.

7. Highlight the value

In client marketing, trust is crucial, but you also need to show how valuable your product is. Detail how your product will assist your customers to accomplish their objectives. Provide excellent customer service and foresee their demands. Use the information you get from your talks with them about their wants to create a pitch that is specifically tailored to meet each one.

Make a presentation specifically for that client that covers every issue they brought up during prior discussions.

8. Have a consultative mindset.

Instead of approaching the prospective customer as a salesman, act as a consultant. Instead of trying to sell the customer anything, you should try to assist them to solve a problem. Be honest and attentive first. Create solutions that are specific to the demands of the customer and show flexibility in response to what the client says. Instead of sticking closely to a script, look for innovative alternatives.

Instead of talking, listen more. Once again, your goal is to establish your credibility as a person they can trust with their money rather than attempting to sell them your goods.

9. Be truthful

Being transparent with a customer and not making unattainable promises are key components in building trust. You may do everything right with a customer up until the point of payment, but if they discover you weren't forthright about price and conditions, it might erode the trust you've worked so hard to establish. Make sure contractual and payment terms are clear.

If you are unable to meet a client's requirement, be honest with them about it or provide an alternative solution. Don't claim to be able to solve it in the anticipation of eventually figuring it out.

10. Do not hesitate to change course.

Yeah, you want that first customer desperately, but it doesn't give you the right to act in ways that aren't beneficial to your company. Don't allow prospects to waste your time by being unreliable. Thank them for their time and move on to the next prospect if they want to chat with you all the time but you can't get them to take the next step.

Establish a strict deadline, thank the client for their time, and then move on. Keep in mind that your time is worth more than any one prospect. Go on to the next one because there will be more.

Keep that customer satisfied after the transaction.

Don't disregard continued customer maintenance once you get that client. It is useless to persuade the initial consumer to give you money just to have them want a refund thereafter. Make sure your product is outstanding and your customer service keeps them satisfied because if that occurs, you're back where you started.

This is where client management software might be useful. It will help you stay organized and monitor client interactions so you can make sure there are no problems following a transaction. Try out some of the best software solutions; you could be astonished at how it affects your conversion rate.

Chapter 4:Turn conversations into relationship and revenue

To gain from networked connections, adopt a networking attitude.

Every day, chances to interact with others present themselves. Yet, making deliberate business relationships demands more attention and a mentality that results in a strategy. Entrepreneurs who succeed embrace these convictions:

I need aid. I can't know all there is to know about starting and running a successful company. Even what I don't know is unknown to me. There have been a lot of individuals before me.

No amount of money, ability, or even energy will ever be sufficient to meet all of my needs. To learn how to stretch, I may draw on the expertise of others. Entrepreneurs like supporting one another.

A multifaceted and inclusive approach to hiring will help my firm expand more quickly. I won't get there by speaking to just those who resemble me.

Human interactions are reciprocal. Both sides must grasp the advantages for relationships to succeed. Integrity and trust are essential. While it doesn't happen in every business relationship, many do.

Transform relationships into collaboration

Two people are more likely to bond when they have something in common. Living on the same street or waiting in line at a busy coffee shop might be coincidences. Perhaps from the same interests, such as via membership in a professional association or a common university. Even the famed six degrees of separation with a coworker or friend's family or acquaintances might serve as the starting point. In this case, looking for chances to turn these everyday life connections into productive business partnerships may be transformational for both a company and an entrepreneur. Make communicating with people inside the business ecosystem a simple and automatic part of your everyday routine by implementing these suggestions.

Get to know the local lender. Deal with CPAs and lawyers who focus on helping startup businesses. They may serve as a conduit for contacts with like-minded businesses in the neighborhood in addition to being geared to your requirements.

Become a judge at collegiate business plan contests or offer to provide a guest lecture in business school seminars. Through these actions, a business may build crucial relationships with a talent for internships and new hiring.

Take the initiative in dialogues that develop bridges with others who are not technicians, engineers, or scientists. people who are 20 years your junior or younger. individuals with radically unrelated backgrounds or professions. You'll gain knowledge and discover fresh connections.

Build relationships with racially and ethnically diverse groups to recruit talent that will help businesses perform better than their competitors. Entrepreneurs who simply use their networks and connections are more likely to employ individuals who share their perspectives and experiences. The approach is unsuccessful. The commercial case for diversity and inclusion is reportedly stronger than ever, according to McKinsey. Businesses with the highest levels of ethnic diversity are 35% more likely to have revenue streams that are above average. Teams with more diversity are the result of a concerted search for varied applicants throughout the recruiting process. Local startups provide the following advice:

Make contact with neighborhood grassroots groups and associations where women and minorities are overrepresented. Attend more than a few events. Befriend people. Follow up after exchanging business cards. Become entangled.

Even if you are not hiring right away, go to job fairs that seek candidates from racially and ethnically diverse neighborhoods as well as historically Black institutions and universities.

Startup studios, organizations that promote economic growth, and accelerators serve as a hub for the entrepreneurial community's access to services and activities. Many cater to a wide spectrum of entrepreneurs as well as varied sectors and markets. You join other people's networks when you get to know them. Through this two-way procedure, you could be in a position to mentor or advise someone else.

Get to know people in the venture world and make allies before your firm requires funding.

While your company is still in the idea phase, start developing your contacts to money. You may be surprised by how eager investors are to impart their knowledge to tenacious inventors and businesspeople.

Create a business strategy that aligns funding needs with company milestones. Determine the venture firms and angel investors that finance your sector's development. Make introductions by using your network. Show consideration for their time. Stay teachable. Pose sensible queries. Maintain contact.

municipal authorities. Successful businesspeople are always searching for the next generation of leadership, often including cash-strapped businesses eager to give back. Participate in that wave.

Capital comes later; mentoring comes first.

Your board of directors: The ideal formal partnership

The finest support any entrepreneur can have is a knowledgeable, involved board of directors. The most successful boards support the organization's financial and strategic objectives. The legal makeup of the business determines whether a board of directors is required. The statute establishes the duties of boards of directors. By initially establishing a board of advisers, you may learn how to develop a board and collaborate with a board of directors.

Assemble a select group of knowledgeable advisers early on in the development of the organization. They could come from business, academia, or a successful startup. Choose three or four dependable friends who can help. I've always believed that business owners who ask for guidance before inviting others to serve as advisers create stronger boards.

Choose people with various connections and skill sets from your own. If technology is your area of expertise, choose a partner with strong financial or marketing skills. Avert friends and relatives. It's crucial to build ties with VCs before they invest since investors will want board seats.

Be honest about your expectations with possible advisers and with yourself. Advisory boards have no decorative use. One person at a time, form teams. Check to make sure there aren't any conflicts of interest. There are many chances for networking. An entrepreneur can choose to spend every waking hour of every day socializing instead of validating the market, generating leads, or prototyping. That is not the goal. Assets that are not recorded on the balance sheet are intentional connections.

Some business owners find relationship development to be natural, while others find it uncomfortable. In any case, the attitudes and actions that foster great interpersonal relationships also foster successful corporate cultures.

Chapter 5: **Master the first meeting**

1. Be on time. To avoid wasting other people's time as they wait for you to come for a meeting, always be on time. Don't come too early; a few minutes is great, but more than that makes everyone uncomfortable by interfering with other people's ability to get ready for the meeting. If you arrive early, find something else to do. For example, you may straighten your hair, grab a sip of water, or wash your hands in cold water to keep them from sweating when shaking hands.

2. Don't just wear what you would normally wear to work; dress correctly. Unless it is drastically outside of industry standards, a professional business suit in dark hues is suitable for meeting with representatives from other organizations. Choose a solid or pinstriped shirt, and males should choose a matching tie. Present a nice, tidy image by wearing freshly ironed clothes, shoes, and nails.

3. Before the meeting begins, strike up a conversation to reduce tensions. Make an effort to get to know the other participants. Pay attention to the dialogue and the personal nuances that might help you establish a lasting bond with the other guests. Avoid checking your emails or chewing gum during the meeting.

4. Do preliminary research. Learn about the company's most recent successes, upcoming initiatives, and important projects by reviewing business papers and online information. Compose one or two major inquiries and goals that you wish to discuss at the meeting in advance.

5. Find a balance by providing pertinent remarks while limiting your speaking time. Avoid interjecting while others are speaking. Avoid fighting; it is not suitable to settle personal disputes in a group business gathering. Make all of your encounters professional, focused, and brief. Avoid having rambling conversations or

deviating off-topic. If you called the meeting, make an agenda and follow it, kindly guiding other attendees back on track if they stray too far from it.

How to Have a Conversation in an Official Setting

Anxiety and Positivity

When you first meet someone, give them a solid handshake and a friendly grin. Try relaxation methods, such as breathing from your mouth and out your nose, if you have anxiety during business meetings and chats. If caffeine-rich drinks make you jittery or cause you to speak too quickly, slow down when you speak. Anxiety might convey to others that you are unconfident and unreliable.

Active listening and empathy

Put yourself in the shoes of other coworkers and consider issues from their perspectives to practice empathy. By focusing on what is being said as well as body language and voice tone, practice active listening. Avoid interjecting and pay attention to what is being said.

Conflicts

Take a step back and breathe deeply if you find yourself in a combative or angry debate. Make sure you comprehend what your coworkers are attempting to say and what they mean. If you're unclear, ask your coworkers to elaborate or rephrase what you believe they're saying before asking if it's accurate. Be aggressive but refrain from making charges. Use facts to back up your assertions when you are advocating a certain viewpoint.

Various Views

Modify your perspective on what others think. Recognize that meetings have a purpose and that everyone in the office is working together to achieve that purpose. Being optimistic will alter how you respond to opposing viewpoints. Don't undervalue or be gloomy about diverse people's views; rather, respect their value. Maintain meeting notes that list the many suggestions the group makes. The team might research several concepts and present them at the subsequent business meeting. This spotlights and incorporates various team members, fostering a sense of importance and involvement among them.

Silence

Don't be frightened of stillness; capitalize on it. Give thoughtful consideration to each inquiry and concern. Prepare your speech in advance by thinking it through. Consider potential issues and how you could handle them in advance of meetings in the future.

How to Interact at a Workplace Group Meeting

1. Pay close attention and take notes. Make sure you comprehend the facts being discussed by taking a minute. Any queries you have should be written down so you can answer them later. Many meeting planners provide time for queries and issues.

2. To demonstrate that you are paying attention, make brief eye contact with each person who speaks. Have an open posture to convey that you are receptive to fresh ideas. Avoid doing anything that might distract the speaker and the meeting attendees, such as crossing your arms, tapping your pens, and swinging your chair.

3. Wait until speakers have finished speaking before adding your own. When you have nothing pertinent or significant to say, refrain from speaking. Talk loudly enough for others to comprehend you. Instead of skirting the issue, be straightforward with your responses and back up all of your thoughts with evidence.

4. Ensure that all parties comprehend what is being said. If you are providing intricate concepts or analyses, use schematics to support the content, such as charts and presentations.

5. Remain friendly. Keep in mind that it is just business. Even if other attendees are acting

disrespectfully at the meeting, refrain from using offensive comments. Keep your best conduct up.

Establish rapport and trust

Reliability

Your customers' perceptions of your capacity to provide high-quality work are distinct from their perceptions of your ability to do that work as promised, on schedule, and within the specified budget. It all comes down to dependability: do they feel secure in your presence?

"Your team is working well and making excellent progress," was a wonderful example of an agency that can be relied upon in our short case study. But, your customer was unaware of this since no one had attempted to inform them.

As a result, the client's confidence in you quickly diminished since they began to doubt your dependability. Oops!

Intimacy

With a customer, stakeholder, or another business contact, there are three different degrees of intimacy:

Professional closeness is a state of comfort where your contact may discuss sensitive information.
Intimate closeness occurs when they are comfortable enough with you to share a bit about themselves and their future goals.
The ultimate degree of intimacy is intimate closeness, where your contact will feel comfortable disclosing their anxieties.
A fundamental component of trust is intimacy because of the dangers it entails. You could abuse the information they provide, like in the case when your customer expresses worries about other agencies.

Self-Orientation
Trust's last element acts against other people. The authors demonstrate this in the denominator of their calculation since it corrodes confidence. The degree to which your customers, coworkers,

or stakeholders believe you are operating in your own best interests is known as self-orientation.

Indeed, of course, we all do. Very few of us work just for charitable purposes. Nonetheless, the company or expert that voluntarily rewrites a portion of a client brief for free charge to please their client will do well in this area. In contrast, a commercial manager can charge variation fees each time a customer picks up the phone.

Calculating Trust
First of all, whatever results you get from calculating trust are only suggestive. Second, you can only approach it from the perspective of one stakeholder at a time. Their own experience of your working style will determine how they see your dependability. Regardless of how trustworthy you believe yourself to be, it won't matter.

The writers advise you to estimate and assign a score of 10 to how a customer views you on each of the four categories. Never let yourself believe that you have no self-orientation in their eyes! Avoiding that mistake can also help you avoid unpleasant "division by zero" issues.

If you are completely honest, you'll frequently discover that one or two issues are weakening the whole situation. This will show you where further work is needed to foster trust.

Ways to Increase Trust
How do you then go about establishing trust? Fortunately, Maister, Green, and Galford provide you with a five-stage method for methodically developing trust. The five stages, as they are to be understood by digital project managers, are:

Develop a relationship of trust with the customer or stakeholder whose trust you want. To do this, pick up the phone or, even better, set up a meeting.
Take note of what they are saying. The importance of this outweighs their ability to hear you. Contrary to popular belief, listening establishes credibility better than speaking. Also,

it undoubtedly improves feelings of closeness and self-orientation. If only you could learn to control your lips, it ought to be simpler as well!

Describe your understanding of their issues in a manner that demonstrates how well you comprehend their key problems. This indicates trustworthiness, we-placed connection, and a focus on them and their issues rather than your own.

Imagine what you and them could achieve if you collaborated. Your credibility and low self-orientation stand out in this situation. Also, it is a well-known truth that positivism and optimism draw people in.

Commit to participating in what has to be done as a team. Establish the management checkpoints, reporting, and communication mechanisms that will enable you to prove your dependability.

dive in and add value

1. Better Understand Them

How attentively are you hearing? Are you spending the time required to validate your beliefs about your clients? As consultants, we often believe that we are aware of the desires and thoughts of our customers.

Yet this isn't always the case. Asking customers probing questions and allowing them to communicate is the greatest method to better understand them. Pay attention to what they say.

When we do this with a large enough number of customers, we begin to see any patterns that emerge. And what distinct qualities, aspirations, and goals they each have. All of this important information enables us to provide superior service to our customers and establish our irreplaceability.

2. Better Serve Them

You'll always keep your customer's interests in mind if you develop a mentality of service. You must make a significant change in your way of thinking.

Relationships with clients aren't just about doing business; they're about providing our clients with the best service we can. Your relationships with customers will alter as you internalize this and put it into practice. You'll be more attentive to them and their requirements. You'll find yourself getting more devoted to them and wanting to assist them on a deeper level.

Customers notice this change. They see the change and value it.

3. Provide superior experiences
Every company has a fantastic potential to provide its clients with more memorable experiences. What are you doing to produce those life-changing moments?

4. Aid Them In Achieving Their Objectives
When you comprehend your customer, you may provide them with a variety of supports. If they seek a promotion within their company, you now

knowing of that, may search for methods to assist them to accomplish it.

You may locate possibilities for them to speak a new language if they are eager to do so. You may provide them with tools to help them if they desire to master a new talent.

Their objective might be either professional or personal. It is unimportant. It is important to be aware of their goals so that you can support and assist them in achieving them.

5. Provide Them with Resources
You may provide materials that your customers will appreciate to position yourself as the authority and expert in your field and to maintain that position over time.

This may be done via blog posts, whitepapers, audio interviews, films, manuals, e-books, physical books, online training, and a long list of other mediums.

Your customer will see you as the authority the more relevant stuff you publish. You'll stay at the top of people's minds. It not only helps you with your customer, but it also gives them more reasons to recommend you to others since they are always thinking about you.

Curate News and Content, number six
Being a source of news and material is a fantastic additional strategy to maintain that top-of-mind placement. Send your customers any news items, articles, or other stuff you come across that you think they'll find valuable or interesting.

Due to these two effects:
1) It demonstrates to your customer that you are remaining on top. In comparison to them and your rivals, you are always one step ahead. Your expertise is further supported by this.
2) Customers value your consideration of them. the resources that they may otherwise have missed are being sent because you care enough.

It conveys your concern for them. And they see that.

7. Personalize Your Connection

There is a lot of "conventional" wisdom out there that cites a variety of justifications for why you shouldn't develop a personal bond with a "business" customer.

I think thinking is a faulty and immature process. We are in the connection business as consultants. Buyers choose to work with those they like.

I'm not suggesting that you spend the night at your client's residence or tell your most dramatic high school anecdotes. I'm advising that you seek chances to interact with your customers in person outside of meetings.

Take a stroll with them. Transport them to their next meeting. Have a meal together. even go to their child's baseball game with them.

Since most individuals are on guard when they are in a formal business atmosphere, this strategy is effective. They believe they must project a "corporate" or "serious" image. When you remove them from that setting and place them in a more intimate and cozy one, they start to relax.

Chapter 6:**Using power questions**

The seven crucial inquiries you ask your clientele
What would you like?
People sometimes struggle to respond to this question, but you may be able to bring them there by asking follow-up questions that probe deeper.

The following query follows:

What is preventing you?
We do, in general, understand this as humans. Even if we may be in denial about it, most of the time we are aware of the actions we do that hinder our ability to change or the thoughts and feelings that prevent us from doing so.

What then is stopping you?

That query will prompt your coaching client to dig deep and take a good, hard look at the truth, capital T.

Voici the third query:

What does continuing to hold back cost you?
I doubt that humans often consider the consequences of their behaviors, beliefs, or habits, but when someone is asked, they are forced to take a more responsible look at themselves.

The following question is:

How could you seem any other way?
This inquiry allows them to ponder, Well, I'm at the choice here, as you're probably talking to them about a condition or a situation. How could I arrive any other way?

I recall being quite anxious the one time I had to talk in front of coaches on a big occasion. How do you want to arrive, Rhonda? My husband asked me when I phoned him for assistance.

I stopped and gave it some consideration. I want to come across as a strong, self-assured speaker who is honest and sensitive with my audience while still providing them with something of genuine value.

Their four responses helped to ground me. They restored my sense of well-being and preparedness. I also realized that I could be open and honest with my audience. It's alright that I felt anxious, and I didn't need to attempt to hide it before taking the stage.

The next question is:

What fresh viewpoint might you take on this situation right now?
It may be a complaint when one of our coaching clients expresses how they feel or what they believe about something. There is nothing wrong with the raw sensation if that is what it is.

I encourage my clients to express their true emotions.

What's a fresh viewpoint you might take on it right now in response to that raw information?

You're urging them to take charge of the problem and get perspective from a great height. Consider things from the perspective of the other party. or from the perspective of their best selves.

What is the most important action you could do right now, according to the sixth question?
When one of our customers is stuck, it's often because they are hesitant or frightened to act, and when you add the word "meaningful" before action, it changes the way they see it.

They could find writing in a diary meaningful. Alternatively, it can be conversing with you or another person. Choosing not to do anything at all and going differently can be meaningful to them.

This is the seventh query:

What new routines are you going to start today? The power of habits in our lives and the lives of our customers is astounding.

Everyone has terrible habits. If you look at any area of our lives on the life wheel, whether it be money, how we act at work, how we eat, or how we exercise, we all have negative habits in that area.

Everyone has habits that can be strengthened, and the appropriate habits can be effective.

Chapter 7:Become your clients person of interest

Maintain contact

We all like being reminded of our existence because it makes us feel significant and valuable. For our customers, it may be a routine phone call to check how the company is doing, what has changed, and what new difficulties have surfaced. Whereas flowers or a foot massage might be a nice approach to show that attention to a loved one. A sound marketing strategy that keeps your business current and top-of-mind should be put in place in addition to routine phone calls or email check-ins.

This marketing strategy could include supporting materials like webcasts, user group meetings, and newsletters. This kind of communication makes it possible for you to foresee potential needs and offer your company's support - before someone else does.

Think of remedies

Here, we're discussing cooperation. Even if you are a software specialist, your customer is an authority in their industry. Work through issues and solutions together, being careful to fully comprehend both their concerns and their desired result. You have access to a wide range of solution options as a software provider. Asking the correct questions and paying close attention to your client's concerns can increase your chances of recommending the best course of action at the appropriate moment.

You may increase the value of your company's services and create long-lasting, mutually beneficial relationships with your customers by acting as a strategic partner to them.

Talk openly

By giving your customers what they want to hear or making promises you can't fulfill, you aren't doing them any favors. Respecting their time, money, and technological commitment, you should establish reasonable expectations for the solutions you're recommending and the potential returns on their money. While you won't have all the answers, if you are open and sincere with your customers at all times, they will appreciate you. Furthermore, keep in mind that it's okay to refuse.

Your honesty in this area will go a long way since you can't handle every problem people bring to you.

Grow to be essential

You don't just effectively complete each assignment you land; you become vital to your customer. You develop a reputation for being necessary by always looking for and advising methods for them to use software to address fresh business difficulties.

Maintain your knowledge of current issues, techniques, and trends.

The smartest individuals don't claim to know everything; instead, they seek advice from those who are authorities in their areas of study and then transform that knowledge into fresh concepts, new paths, and creativity. As a software supplier, you provide value for your customers when you present them with fresh concepts and options based on your analysis of their company and the competing commercial offerings in their industry.

They will respect your connection more and turn to you first as their go-to expert supplier the more problem-solutions you can supply for them. Remember that your customers are continuously receiving marketing communications from other companies touting related goods and services.

chapter 8:**Keep your client for life**

1) Always put the second sale first

With every consumer, the first sale is usually the most difficult and costliest. But, the second is the one that matters the most.

The second sale serves as evidence that you kept your commitments from the previous transaction.

You go out every day and sell people your promises in return for their money. You guarantee that using your product or service will provide them advantages over their competition.

They are endorsing your products and certifying that you kept your promises when they return and make another purchase from you.

2) Referrals and repeat business are almost free

Ten times simpler than new sales to new consumers are resales to happy customers. One-tenth of the time and effort needed to complete a resale.

Because of this, the majority of successful businesses gauge their performance by how often their clients make further purchases.

A warm call is fifteen times harder to sell to than a reference from a happy client. One-fifth of the time, money, and effort go into selling a recommendation. Indeed, if you have a solid recommendation, the sale is done 90% of the time even before you enter the store.

3) Establish A Golden Chain Of Recommendations And Satisfaction
Create a "golden chain of referrals" by asking everyone to suggest you to other interested prospects once you've closed the transaction and the consumer is satisfied.

Ask with confidence. Expectantly ask. Always politely ask clients, even those who aren't clients, whether they may recommend you to someone else.

Assure those you ask for a recommendation that you won't place any pressure on the individual they give you their name. Unless they are certain that the friend or acquaintance they are recommending won't be upset or furious with them for providing you their name, people are cautious to provide recommendations.

4) Create word-of-mouth marketing
The most effective way for you to get recommendations in today's cutthroat industry is by getting your satisfied clients to spread the word about you.

Your goal is to turn your existing customers into a sales force by having them promote you to new potential clients.

Do you want to learn how to inspire people to do this action?

By providing them with exceptional customer service, you may encourage your consumers to make purchases from you.

Speed is always the most crucial component of excellent customer service. A crucial indicator of how many recommendations you are likely to get is your ability to respond quickly to questions, issues, and requests.

To get recommendations, quick and consistent customer service is crucial.

Use the marketing golden rule...

Treat your clients in the same manner that you would want to be served by your suppliers. Treat your clients the same way you would your husband, mother, or best friend.

go above and above.

Do more often than is required.

5) Dispute The Fundamental Issue
After years of research, Fred Reichheld of Bain & Company concluded that there was only one question that was more predictive of customer satisfaction and referral business than any other single question.

He referred to it as the crucial issue.

Would you suggest us to others based on your interaction with us?

The ultimate degree of customer satisfaction is when a consumer is eager to refer you to others.

Most frequently, if you build a solid connection with noncustomers, they will like and trust you so much that they will suggest you to others even if they do not purchase themselves.

6) Request reviews at all times

You may pose the following question after the sales conversation:

Would you recommend us to others, on a scale of one to ten?

Of course, a 10 is what you're aiming for.

When your clients rate you 10 out of ten:

They'll develop into a "raving fan."
They will support the brand and the client.
They will urge all of their friends to make purchases from you.
So what if you get a grade of seven or eight instead of ten?

You thank them for their response before asking what they need to do to get a ten from them the next time.

Ask your clients often, "How are we doing?" and "How can we improve for the future?"

The best-paid and most effective salesmen are those that build a clientele of loyal, repeat clients who purchase from them quickly and easily, are less price sensitive, and serve as the cornerstone of any company's expansion.

7) Develop a Better Customer Service Plan
Create a customer sales and service plan that will help you attract and retain lifelong clients.

This kind of client care is not haphazard. Everyone that interacts with your clients must be carefully planned for, discussed, and trained.

All reputable salespeople and companies are renowned for their excellent customer service. All reputable salespeople and companies are renowned for their excellent customer service.

8) Do Something
What one thing can you do with every client or potential client to make them want to recommend you to other potential clients?

Identify the one activity or behavior that any employee in your firm may engage in that might lower referral business and customer satisfaction. How quickly could you get rid of it?

Participating in a 37-second sales skills exam is one step you can take to determine precisely what you need to do to improve your sales and customer happiness.